The U.S. MARINE CORPS

HUNTER KEETER

WORLD ALMANAC® LIBRARY

Please visit our web site at: www.worldalmanaclibrary.com
For a free color catalog describing World Almanac® Library's list of high-quality books
and multimedia programs, call 1-800-848-2928 (USA) or 1-800-387-3178 (Canada).
World Almanac® Library's fax: (414) 332-3567.

Library of Congress Cataloging-in-Publication Data

Keeter, Hunter.
    The U.S. Marine Corps / by Hunter Keeter.
        p. cm. — (America's armed forces)
    Includes bibliographical references and index.
    ISBN 0-8368-5683-X (lib. bdg.)
    ISBN 0-8368-5690-2 (softcover)
    1. United States. Marine Corps—Juvenile literature. I. Title: United States Marine Corps.
    II. United States. Marine Corps. III. Title. IV. Series.
    VE23.K43 2004
    359.9'6'0973—dc22   2004042794

First published in 2005 by
World Almanac® Library
330 West Olive Street, Suite 100
Milwaukee, WI 53212 USA

Copyright © 2005 by World Almanac® Library.

Developed by Amber Books Ltd.
Editor: James Bennett
Designer: Colin Hawes
Photo research: Sandra Assersohn, Natasha Jones
World Almanac® Library editor: Mark Sachner
World Almanac® Library art direction: Tammy West
World Almanac® Library production: Jessica Morris

Picture Acknowledgements
U.S.D.O.D.: cover, 4, 35, 37, 38, 40, 42; Istituto Geografico DeAgostini: 5; TRH Pictures: 6, 8,
9, 10, 15, 22 (USMC), 25, 36 (DOD/USMC); U.S.M.C. Historical Center: 7, 23, 24t, 26, 28, 32;
U.S.M.C. Art Collection: 12, 13, 14, 16, 17, 19, 21; Corbis: 18; U.S. National Archives: 20, 24b,
29, 30, 33; U.S. Naval Academy: 31; Aerospace/Art-Tech: 34.

Printed in Canada

2 3 4 5 6 7 8 9 09 08 07 06 05

About the Author

HUNTER KEETER is a journalist with *Defense Daily*, a leading defense business
publication, and has also contributed to *Sea Power* magazine, a resource of record for
the U.S. Navy, U.S. Marine Corps, and U.S. Coast Guard. Before becoming a writer
he earned an M.A. in Literature and Education from the University of South Carolina
and worked as an archivist and a schoolteacher. He lives in Arlington, Virginia.

Table of Contents

Introduction

Right: Marines have become the U.S. military's "911" force, deployed for action at short notice anywhere in the world. Here an assault vehicle crewman keeps watch in Kosovo in July 1999.

It may be difficult to imagine the United States military without thinking of the Marine Corps, that small, all-purpose force that prides itself on being "a few good men" (and women) ready to serve around the world at a moment's notice. More than 200 years ago, however, the ancestors of today's U.S. Marine Corps might have found it just as difficult to imagine what their service would become. Since its creation, the Marine Corps has gradually defined its place in the U.S. military **arsenal**, and sometimes struggled to protect its very existence from those who thought the Army and Navy could make do without it.

The Marine Corps is one of the five military services in the U.S. Department of Defense and the U.S. Department of Homeland Security. The Marines pride themselves on being distinct from the Navy, Army, Air Force, and Coast Guard as a small, elite force capable of performing many tasks. The Marine Corps has its own aircraft, fighting vehicles, and infantry units. The U.S. Marine Corps is, along with the U.S. Navy, part of the Department of the Navy, a component of the Department of Defense. The Marines are often a first resort when the U.S. government decides to use military power in a crisis.

The Marine Corps has not always held status as a premier fighting force. The need for a Marine Corps was called into question at various times in history because the Army and Navy sometimes did the same types of jobs now performed by the Marines. By the end of the twentieth century, however, the government had come to value an independent Marine Corps. While the Army, Navy, and Air Force are designed to fight and win wars, the Marine Corps has become a flexible organization, capable of fighting alongside troops and also capable of playing a role in U.S. foreign policy, providing humanitarian relief, peacekeeping, and other jobs outside the realm of the violence of war.

By embracing ethnic and gender diversity, the Marine Corps has become, like the other services, an example of the society that bore it. History records a difficult path taken to achieve what Marines today value as a proud heritage. The story of that journey is one of struggling forward through hardship and adventure to take a unique place among the United States' armed forces.

Below: A U.S. Marine as he would have been equipped during the Vietnam War.

Right: The first Marines were tough soldiers and seamen recruited for their ability to fight on land or at sea. These first two battalions of Marines were considered part of the Continental Army.

The first **regiment** of U.S. Marines, the forerunner of today's U.S. Marine Corps, was formed on November 10, 1775, by an act of the Continental Congress. During the Revolutionary War, at a meeting in Philadelphia, Pennsylvania, the Continental Congress resolved that

*Two **battalions** of Marines be raised… that particular care be taken, that no persons be appointed to office, or enlisted into said Battalions, but such as are good seamen, or so acquainted with maritime affairs as to be able to serve to advantage by sea when required…that they be distinguished by the names of the first and second battalions of U.S. Marines, and that they be considered part of the number [of] the continental Army before Boston.*

In the beginning, Marines were to support the Navy and Army in actions that required the use of amphibious troops (soldiers trained to sail aboard Navy ships and then landed ashore to fight). Other tasks included protecting Navy officers aboard ships and suppressing **mutinies**. Often, Marines serving aboard naval vessels were quartered, or housed, between the officers and the crew below deck. The Marines of a ship's complement led naval artillery action while aboard, hence the rank, persisting today, of "gunnery sergeant." In the U.S. military, particularly during the Revolutionary War, Marines served similar purposes that Army troops did when ashore; that is, serving as **infantry** and artillery forces, fighting in the same battles and under the same overall command.

Above: Captain Samuel Nicholas commanded the first Marine regiment in action at New Providence in the Bahamas. He also supported the Continental Army in New Jersey.

The Revolutionary War

The first U.S. Marine battalions were commanded by Captain Samuel Nicholas, who was commissioned an officer by the same Congress that authorized the creation of a Marine regiment. Nicholas was born in Philadelphia to the wife of a Quaker blacksmith. Quakers, a Christian sect also called the Religious Society of Friends, have, since the seventeenth century, been opposed to preparations for war, so it was interesting that Nicholas chose the life of a soldier.

Below: The Marines took part in the first American amphibious assault of the Revolutionary War, capturing British forts and munitions in the Bahamas.

By the end of 1775, Captain Nicholas commanded five companies of Marines. These companies sailed early the next year in a seven-vessel squadron, led by the 24-gun warship *Alfred*. In March 1776, the Marines and sailors of this squadron boarded open boats and rowed ashore, landing on the beach at New Providence, the Bahamas. These troops captured two British forts, Montego and Nassau, in a successful amphibious assault by forces. At New Providence, the action was brief, but decisive. The gunners at Fort Montego fired five of their cannon, but did no harm before the fort was captured, along with 17 guns and more than 1,400 rounds of ammunition. At Fort Nassau, Captain Nicholas sent a message to the British governor of

the Bahamas, requesting him to surrender the keys of the fort. After Nicholas promised them safe conduct upon surrender, the two hundred troops guarding Fort Nassau for the British abandoned the fort, giving it up to Nicholas' shore party without a battle. Among the military equipment seized at Nassau were 71 guns, 15 **mortars**, and more than 15,000 rounds of shot and shell.

The weaponry taken at the two Bahamian forts was the most important goal of the expedition, since, at the start of the Revolutionary War, the Americans had little equipment with which to fight the British army and the Royal Navy, at that time among the most powerful military forces in the world. The guns taken at New Providence were sailed back to Connecticut and delivered to Americans preparing for the battles that would come over the next eight years of war.

After other adventures, Nicholas earned a promotion to the rank of major. He commanded three companies of Marines through the battles at Trenton and Princeton, in New Jersey, alongside General Washington's army. After 1777, Nicholas's Marines' roles were reduced in action until, by 1783, when the Revolutionary War ended with the Treaty of Paris, both the Navy and the Marines were disbanded. Nicholas retired in Philadelphia. He was 46 years old when he died in 1790, and was buried in a Quaker cemetery.

Marine Corps Symbols

The official U.S. Marine Corps colors are scarlet and gold. The seal of the Marines, a "foul anchor" (an anchor with a chain wound around it) surmounted by an eagle, on a globe, has come down from the early days of the service. The anchor symbolizes amphibious duty, the globe symbolizes a worldwide reach, and the eagle represents the strength of the U.S. Marine Corps. Often displayed alongside the seal, the official Marine Corps motto is *Semper Fidelis*, which is a Latin phrase meaning "Ever Faithful."

Above: The modern U.S. Marine Corps is the expeditionary and amphibious fighting arm of the U.S. Department of the Navy.

Right: Born in Virginia in 1776, Presley Neville O'Bannon was to become one of the most famous early Marine Corps leaders.

As the United States grew after it gained independence, its interests in the world also became more complicated. It didn't take long before the government realized the value of maintaining a navy to protect and influence U.S. interests abroad. The Constitution of the United States was ratified (approved) in 1789 and gave Congress the authority to establish a U.S. Navy. More than a decade later, on July 11, 1798, President John Adams officially signed into existence the U.S. Marine Corps. Almost immediately, the Marines were in action.

The Marines and the Pirates

Among the famous Marines of this era was Presley Neville O'Bannon, born in Virginia the year the Declaration of Independence was signed, 1776. Promoted to the rank of first lieutenant, he was given a special mission in the spring of 1805, when the United States was at war with the Barbary Pirates of the North African coast. The Barbary Pirates were groups of men who roamed the waters between the Atlantic Ocean and the Mediterranean Sea, preying upon merchant ships. The crew of the USS *Philadelphia*, a Navy ship that had run aground in a storm off Tripoli, the capital of Libya, had been imprisoned by Pasha Yousuf Karamali, who commanded some of the pirates demanding **tribute** from the U.S. government.

O'Bannon helped carry out a raid on Yousuf's fortress to rescue *Philadelphia*'s crew. Yousuf's exiled brother, Hamet, led Arab horsemen, along with O'Bannon's seven Marines and a combined force of U.S. Navy sailors and Greek and Turkish soldiers. They marched 500 miles (800 kilometers) across the Libyan Desert to seize Yousuf's fortress and a nearby harbor **bastion** in a short, fierce fight. As a reward for his bravery, Hamet gave O'Bannon a Mameluke saber similar to the kind carried by some desert tribesmen. This sword is the same type of blade now worn by modern Marine officers when in dress uniform.

The War of 1812

During the War of 1812 (1812–1815), the U.S. Marine Corps had roles to play at sea aboard Navy ships and ashore defending the cities of Washington, D.C., and, more successfully, New Orleans, Louisiana. The War of 1812 had its

Right: Marines and sailors serving with U.S. Marine Lieutenant Presley Neville O'Bannon helped capture the fortress at Tripoli, deciding a key battle in the war against the Barbary Pirates of North Africa.

origins in the British practice of impressment, which is the seizure of U.S. seamen for service in the Royal Navy. The British claimed that they were only seizing British citizens who avoided their military duty by "hiding out" on U.S. ships. The truth, however, was that British and U.S. citizens alike were seized. One source estimates that as many as 6,000 U.S. citizens were impressed during this time. President James Madison requested a declaration of war to protect U.S. ships on the high seas and to stop the British from impressing U.S. sailors. Neither Britain nor the United States was particularly well prepared to fight this war, however, and the conflict eventually ended in a stalemate.

Battles at Home and Elsewhere

During the nineteenth century, the Marine Corps continued to work alongside the U.S. Army. From 1835 through 1841, the Marines and the Army fought in Georgia and Florida to force the Seminole and Creek peoples to move from their ancestral lands onto federal reservations hundreds of miles west. The Seminoles and Creeks resisted, and there was war. The Marines and Army fought again together during the Mexican War (1846–1848).

"... TO THE SHORES OF TRIPOLI"

Territory was one of the primary issues behind this war. Mexico once had control of lands that are now the states of Texas, Arizona, New Mexico, and Colorado, among others, but an inability to maintain an economic foothold in those areas as well as the United States' desire to expand soon led to war. At the National Palace in Mexico City, built atop the palace of Aztec emperor Montezuma, Marines raised the U.S. flag and inspired the first verse of the now-famous Marine Corps Hymn, "From the halls of Montezuma, to the shores of Tripoli."

Marines were also present during the bloodiest period of U.S. history, the Civil War (1861–1865). When nine Southern states voted to **secede** from the Union in 1861, forming the short-lived Confederate States of America, the U.S. Marine Corps was torn apart; almost half of Marine officers resigned their commissions to join the Confederate cause. U.S. and Confederate marine units supported larger army forces during the war. For example, a combined force of U.S. Marines, sailors, and soldiers participated in the assault on Fort Fisher, North Carolina, in January 1865. This action was the last major amphibious operation of the Civil War with more than 3,000 federal troops and more than

Left: Between 1835 and 1841, U.S. Marines and U.S. Army troops served together in a bloody war against Seminole and Creek Indians in Florida.

Above: U.S. Marines served under U.S. Army Colonel Robert E. Lee in the capture of **abolitionist** militant John Brown at the Harper's Ferry federal arsenal, Virginia, in 1859. After Virginia seceded from the Union in 1861, Lee became commander of Confederate forces in the Civil War.

40 U.S. ships assaulting the fort's 1,500-man strong Confederate garrison. Almost 2,000 troops were killed in the fighting.

After the Civil War the U.S. Marine Corps, which had increased in size to include more than 4,000 troops, again supported the U.S. Navy in action overseas. The United States was expanding its diplomatic and commercial interests, particularly over the Caribbean Sea and in South America, as well as across the Pacific Ocean to Korea, China, and the South Pacific islands.

Late in the 1890s, the United States went to war with Spain to help people in Cuba and the Philippine Islands win their independence. It was during this conflict that Marines demonstrated the value of using troops ashore to signal Navy ships where to direct their artillery fire. At a place called Cuzco Well,

Cuba, when a nearby U.S. Navy ship, the USS *Dolphin*, used its guns against Spanish and Cuban forces, Marines were caught in the crossfire. Sergeant John H. Quick used a signal flag to alert the *Dolphin* and redirect its fire against the enemy.

Above: At Guantanamo Bay, Cuba—now the site of a major U.S. naval base—Marines were the first troops ashore during the 1898 Spanish–American War.

The Marine Corps Hymn

From the Halls of Montezuma to the Shores of Tripoli,
We fight our country's battles
In the air, on land, and sea.
First to fight for right and freedom,
And to keep our honor clean,
We are proud to claim the title of United States Marine.

Right: U.S. Marines joined forces with troops from several nations defending the foreign **legation** quarter in Beijing, China in 1900–01.

By 1900, U.S. Marines were **deployed** across the world, including the Far East. In China, a number of countries (including Japan, Germany, Great Britain, and France, among others) held possession of some Chinese land and resources. A Chinese organization called the Boxers led a violent campaign to oust these foreigners from Chinese territory in what became known as the Boxer Rebellion. Almost 500 U.S. Marines joined a multinational military force to defend the foreign consulates in China, marching on Beijing in 1900 and 1901. One of the Marines best remembered from this conflict was Private Daniel Daly, who became one of only two Marines ever awarded the Congressional Medal of Honor twice, the most prestigious military award the United States government can bestow. Daly won his first Congressional Medal of Honor for bravery during the Boxer Rebellion. He was not a large man—only 5 feet 6 inches (1.7 meters) tall and 132 pounds (60 kilograms), according to U.S. Marine Corps records—but Daly had a lot of fighting spirit. Daly single-handedly held off a Chinese attack using his rifle and its bayonet to defend a wall near the U.S. **legation** in Beijing until reinforcements arrived. He won a second Congressional Medal of Honor fighting bandits in Haiti in 1915.

World War I

World War I (then known as the Great War) broke out in Europe in 1914, but it was years before the Marines saw action, again alongside the U.S. Army, in the U.S. Expeditionary Force. In 1917, that force joined the Allies (including Australia, Canada, France, Great Britain, Russia, and South Africa) fighting Germany, the Austro-Hungarian Empire, and Ottoman Turkey in the trenches of Flanders and in France. The Marines served under Army Major General John J. "Black Jack" Pershing and were tenacious fighters, as was demonstrated at the Battle of Belleau Wood in June 1918. The Germans were stopped at Belleau Wood and were thrown back onto their lines with determination by a force of Marines that,

Below: As the United States abandoned its policy of isolationism in 1917, U.S. Marines were sent to Europe as part of the American Expeditionary Force. Eye-catching posters like this one helped the Marine Corps attract many recruits.

FIRST IN THE FIGHT~ ALWAYS FAITHFUL~ BE A U.S. MARINE!

once having gained the cover of the woods, relied on its small-unit tactical capability (the ability to organize and fight in small groups, working together to combat a larger force) and rifle marksmanship to wear down the Germans. According to a popular legend in the Corps, it is because of aggressive Marine assaults at Belleau Wood that the Germans began to refer to Marines as *der Teufelhunden* — "the Devil Dogs." The Marines have held onto this nickname ever since.

After the War

The Marines emerged from World War I with a new role. They had become shock troops, able to storm **fortifications** and overwhelm adversaries by main force—something that **light infantry** is not usually expected to do. Marines also took on some new capabilities, with airplanes and heavier guns now in their arsenal. Eventually, these new ideas and technologies came together with traditional Marine naval capability to build the kind of amphibious, "combined arms" force familiar to the U.S. Marine Corps of today. A fleet exercise was held in 1924, during which the Marine Corps tested for the first time the use of amphibious assault vehicles (tanks that could swim), troop-landing craft, airplanes, and naval bombardment. This exercise demonstrated a new approach to war in which amphibious assault was seen as a way to establish advance naval bases during a sea campaign. These efforts were rewarded during the 1940s and the greatest peril the world had yet faced, World War II.

In the years that followed World War I, there were also some changes in the makeup of the Marine Corps. One of the biggest of these changes came in August 1918, when Opha Mae Johnson became the first woman to enlist in the U.S. Marine Corps. Women were allowed to

The Marine Corps Bulldog Mascot

After the Battle of Belleau Wood, the Marine Corps in 1916 adopted the English Bulldog as a symbol. The dog first appeared on recruiting posters featuring the German *der Teufelhunden* (Devil Dogs) nickname they had earned during World War I. English Bulldogs, though small, are known for their fierce, toothy appearance and reputed tenacity.

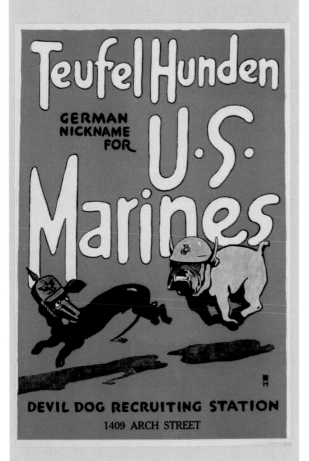

enlist in the Corps as clerical workers under the slogan, "free a Marine to fight." The reasoning was that female recruits could perform administrative duties at home so the men could fight at the front lines. When the war ended, however, the conservative viewpoint that women had no place in the service returned. In 1919, all women were ordered out of the Marine Corps and weren't allowed to come back until 1943 during World War II. Five years later, in 1948, Congress formally allowed women to be integrated into the armed forces and ordered they could become part of the active Marine Corps.

Chapter 4
The Marine Corps in World War II

Right: A U.S. Marine machine-gun team advances on Guadalcanal in 1942. The Pacific Theater island-hopping campaign of World War II tested the limits of Marine amphibious tactics.

On December 7, 1941, a successful Japanese surprise attack on the military bases of Hawaii propelled the United States into World War II. The Marine Corps' airplanes situated near Pearl Harbor Naval Station were almost all destroyed in the attack by Japanese bombers. The United States immediately declared war on Japan, and from that day until the end of the war in August 1945, the Marine Corps fought against Japan over control of the largest ocean—the Pacific—and some of the toughest terrain in the world.

Dark Days

Early in the war against Japan, the United States faced dark days, with losses at Wake Island in 1941, and at Bataan in the Philippines in 1942. The British and the Australians had been pushed back from territories in Southeast Asia, and the Japanese advance seemed unstoppable. By the middle of 1942, however, the Japanese had begun to suffer setbacks of their own, including at the Battle of Midway in June, where four Japanese navy fleet aircraft carriers were destroyed. From this point on, the Japanese were forced to fight a defensive war at sea.

Between August 1942 and February 1943, the U.S. and Royal Australian navies, backing a landing force of U.S. Marines, fought to conquer and hold Guadalcanal Island. U.S. Navy and Australian ships dueled with Japanese counterparts in the aptly named Iron Bottom Sound to the north of Guadalcanal. A large Marine Corps force went ashore using landing boats and "amphibian tractors," called AMTRACs (tracked vehicles that could move through the water like armored boats and crawl like tanks up onto the beach). Eventually, the United States secured the island against the Japanese.

Marines and Army units in the Pacific had special weapons, such as the M2 portable flamethrower. Japanese fortifications combined natural elements, such as caves, trees, and jungle vegetation, with dugouts and other structures. Tough bunkers built of reinforced concrete, sand, and logs guarded beach approaches

Below: Before World War II, the Marines experimented with amphibious warfare, particularly during the 1920s and 1930s, when the basic tactics and hardware were designed and tested.

THE MARINES HAVE LANDED

on Betio Island of the Tarawa Atoll in November 1943 when a force of Marines landed. The Japanese had prepared trenches and tunnels across the island, connecting their defenses into a formidable network. Portable flamethrowers in the hands of Marine combat engineers (troops trained to use explosives, clear obstacles, and disable mines), backed by riflemen, burned the Japanese out of their fortifications and drove back a counterattack.

The End of the War

Leading up to the final assault on Okinawa, an island in southwestern Japan, was some of the fiercest fighting of World War II, between February and

Ending Discrimination

Above: Navajo "code talkers" operating a portable radio set in the jungles of Bougainville in the Solomons during 1943.

In June 1941, about six months before the United States became involved in World War II, President Franklin Delano Roosevelt signed an executive order that said:

All departments of the government, including the Armed Forces, shall lead the way in erasing discrimination over color or race.

With that order, the government took the first steps away from a tradition of having African Americans serve only in separate or segregated units, usually led by white officers. In the Navy, blacks had served alongside whites aboard ships. In the Marine Corps, blacks were segregated into composite defense battalions, trained to use coastal artillery, anti-aircraft guns, and tanks to defend naval bases.

Other Americans from different cultural backgrounds also served in the Marine Corps during World War II. Probably the most famous cultural group in the service at this time were the Navajo (Dineh) Indians who served as "code talkers," using their unwritten language as the basis for a code that allowed Marines to communicate on their radios without being understood by the Japanese.

March 1945, when Allied forces approached the Japanese mainland. In the battle most commemorated by the U.S. Marine Corps, almost 6,800 U.S. troops and more than 20,000 Japanese were killed fighting over the island fortress of Iwo Jima. Capturing Iwo Jima was an important goal for the Allies, as the island's three airfields eventually provided emergency landing facilities for U.S. Army Air Force B-29 bombers returning from raids on Japan. Japanese

Above: U.S. Marines used M2 flamethrowers to destroy Japanese machine-gun nests and infantry hard points on Iwo Jima in 1945.

Above: U.S. Marine Corps F4U Corsairs over Okinawa.

Below: Raising the Stars and Stripes atop Mount Suribachi marked a turning point. While six more months of bitter fighting lay ahead, the capture of Japanese home territory signaled that the end was in sight.

resistance to the Marine invasion of Iwo Jima has been described as "fanatical," because the Japanese viewed Iwo Jima as part of their homeland. Determined Japanese forces on Iwo Jima defended the island with machine-gun emplacements and a tunnel-and-bunker system covering key high ground, such as the volcanic Mount Suribachi to the south.

In the first day of fighting, more than 500 Marines were killed and almost 2,000 wounded. A heavy naval and air bombardment had failed to destroy the Japanese fortifications on the island. By the fourth day of the battle, a Marine patrol and two U.S. Navy hospital corpsmen (sailors trained as medics to accompany the infantry and treat the wounded in battle), after a fierce bombardment by ships' guns and airplanes, climbed to the top of Mount Suribachi. Using a section of metal pipe, six Marines and one of the corpsmen raised a U.S. flag, a scene captured in the famous *Life* magazine photograph that became the model for the Marine Corps' Iwo Jima Memorial near the national cemetery in Arlington, Virginia. Raising the flag at Mount Suribachi was viewed by Secretary of the Navy James Forrestal as "ensuring there would be a Marine Corps for the next 500 years."

On May 8, 1945, Germany surrendered, ending World War II in Europe. Japan continued to fight. On August 6, 1945, the United States government under President Harry S. Truman used the newly developed atomic bomb to destroy the Japanese city of Hiroshima. The decision to use atomic weapons there, and days later at Nagasaki, the only instances in history when such terrible destruction has been used in war, has become controversial. It is worth remembering that in August 1945 the Japanese were not prepared to surrender, thereby raising the possibility that an invasion of the Japanese homeland, at an uncounted cost in U.S. lives, would become the only way to end the war. Historians generally agree that the use of atomic bombs against Japan was critical to ending World War II.

Lieutenant General Lewis B. "Chesty" Puller

Lieutenant General Lewis B. "Chesty" Puller has been described as one of the toughest Marines in history, winning five Navy Cross medals in combat ranging from Nicaragua, during the 1920s, to the Korean War in the 1950s. During a rainy night on Guadalcanal in October 1942, Puller and his Marines were in a fierce fight, killing more than 1,400 enemy soldiers and capturing more than a dozen truckloads of equipment.

Right: Throughout the Korean War, U.S. Marines, as part of a United Nations force, battled both North Korean and Chinese armies and the bitter cold. Here members of the 1st Marine Division march south from Koto-Ri in December 1950.

After World War II, the Marine Corps and other military services resumed discussions regarding which of the armed forces would be responsible for performing what missions. In 1947, President Truman signed two documents that established the Department of Defense and spelled out the specific roles each uniformed service would play. The National Security Act of 1947 and Executive Order 9877 included the creation of a separate U.S. Air Force and reinforced the role of the Marine Corps. The section of the executive order that addressed naval forces stated that it would be the responsibility of the Department of the Navy to maintain the U.S. Marine Corps for missions, including

The seizure or defense of advanced naval bases and for the conduct of limited land operations; amphibious operations; to provide security detachments…for naval stations and bases.

The Korean War

The United States Marine Corps was put to the test again early in the decade following World War II when a multinational United Nations (U.N.) force was formed to battle North Korean **communist** forces. In 1950, Korean communists in the north invaded South Korea, fighting their way through to the capital city, Seoul. In June 1950, the United Nations called for the communists to halt their advance and return north of the 38th Parallel, the border of North

Master Sergeant Barbara J. Dulinsky

On March 17, 1967, Master Sergeant Barbara J. Dulinsky became the first female Marine to arrive in Vietnam. Dulinsky served with Military Assistance Command, Vietnam, near Saigon. Since the Vietnam War, when 2,700 female Marines were on active duty, the job opportunities for women in the Marine Corps have grown. Other notable Marine women include Colonel Gail M. Reals, who became the first female Marine brigadier general in the 1980s. Today, more than four percent of all Marine officers are women and more than five percent of the enlisted Marine force is female.

Korea. The United States promised to enforce the U.N.'s demand and entered the war in July 1950.

At first, the situation was grim for the U.N. Suffering from limited supplies, conflicting intelligence reports, and, in some cases, inadequate equipment, the U.S. Army's forces fell back from the North Korean attack. Swarms of North Korean infantry overran U.S. and allied forces, driving them south toward the coastal city of Pusan. U.S. Army general Douglas S. MacArthur called on the Marine Corps to accomplish an amphibious landing at Inchon, far to the north and east of the embattled U.N. force at Pusan. MacArthur's plan was to split the North Korean force by opening a new line of fighting behind the communist advance. In the late 1940s, some senior officials at the Department of Defense had argued there would never again be such a large-scale amphibious operation as that seen during the Pacific island campaigns of World War II. The Inchon landing would prove these critics wrong.

Below: In September 1950, with surprise and speed on their side, U.S. Marines mount the seawall at Inchon to break the Pusan Perimeter stalemate and turn the tide of the Korean War in favor of U.N. forces.

On September 15, 1950, the 1st Marine **Division** landed at Inchon against a 30-foot (9-m) tide, mud flats, and a challenging urban terrain. Supported by naval airpower, Marine infantry fought through North Korean machine-gun fire to breach a seawall and gain entry into the city. U.S. and British warships used their heavy guns to blast enemy forces opposing the waves of allied landing craft coming ashore. After the amphibious landing force captured Inchon, a nearby airfield fell to U.N. forces, and, within two weeks, the Army was able to break out of its stronghold at Pusan and fight north to recapture Seoul. The fighting in Korea would go on until 1953, as Chinese and Soviet Union forces became directly involved. Almost three-quarters of the communist Chinese Peoples' Liberation Army infantry force became involved in the Korean War, with more than 2 million troops fighting U.N. forces. The Soviets trained the North Korean

Above: An ordnance handling crew loads high-explosive rockets onto the wing of an F4U Corsair in Korea.

Senator John H. Glenn, Jr.

Ohio Senator John H. Glenn, Jr., was a Marine aviator who, during the Korean War, shot down three MiG fighter jets over Korea. Later, during the Mercury Space Program, on February 20, 1962, Glenn became the first American to orbit Earth, in the spacecraft *Friendship 7*. He was elected to the U.S. Senate in 1974.

Right: U.S. Marine fighter pilot John H. Glenn flew "exchange" missions with the U.S. Air Force during the Korean War. Here he stands beside the battle-damaged tail of his F9F Panther jet. The plane had more than 700 holes in it from enemy antiaircraft artillery fire.

army and also had a large force of advisors based in China. Between 1950 and 1953, the Soviet Union provided North Korea with a number of jet fighter **regiments** and their supporting units, directly engaging United Nations strike aircraft flying bombing missions above the 38th Parallel. The Soviet force fighting in Korea included nine fighter aviation divisions (totaling more than 900 aircraft serving in Korea over a period of three years); four ground-based anti-aircraft artillery divisions; and technical support and communications units.

The Soviet government claimed 30 of its pilots were confirmed air aces (pilots who shot down more than five aircraft) during the Korean War.

The ranks of U.S. Marine Corps pilots from the Korean War also boasted their share of aviation heroes, including ace Lt. Col. John F. Bolt, who shot down six MiG fighters. Marine pilot—and later astronaut and U.S. senator from Ohio— John H. Glenn had the nickname "MiG Mad Marine" painted on the fuselage of the F-86 fighter jet he flew while serving on exchange duty with the U.S. Air Force during the conflict.

The Korean War, which resulted in maintaining the borders between North Korea and South Korea, was the first major clash of a much larger and longer-lasting conflict between the Western powers and those of the communist **bloc**. The Korean War began as a "police action" under the aegis of the United Nations, though the confrontation became a violent, if undeclared, war between Western powers and Chinese and Soviet communist forces. The larger conflict was called the Cold War (1945–1991), as it was not characterized by officially declared combat between the Soviet Union and the West. Fighting in places like Korea, however, characterized this 50-year-long struggle.

In Korea, the Marines used helicopters, a relatively new technology at the time, to perform "vertical envelopment," wherein an infantry unit is airlifted over an enemy force and replaced on the ground to fight around and behind it.

The U.S. Naval Academy's Marine Midshipmen

U.S. Marine Corps officers may be trained as midshipmen at the United States Naval Academy in Annapolis, Maryland. Annapolis, a small city on the shores of the Chesapeake Bay, has, since 1845, been the home of the long-standing traditions of the Naval Academy and its history of producing the leaders of the maritime services.

Left: The U.S. Naval Academy schools 1,200 midshipmen annually in 19 fields of study, including engineering, science and mathematics, and the humanities.

The ability of helicopters to change the way war was fought was readily apparent in the next fight facing the Marine Corps, in a place called Vietnam, in Southeast Asia.

The Vietnam War

In 1965 Marines became involved in a civil war between forces loyal to the U.S.-backed government of South Vietnam and communist rebels backed by North Vietnamese leader Ho Chi Minh. By 1968, the United States had become fully committed to this war and faced heavy fighting with both North Vietnamese regular forces and Viet Cong guerillas loyal to Ho Chi Minh. In 1968, during the Tet holiday (Chinese New Year), communist forces launched a major offensive operation into the south, attempting to overrun the South Vietnamese and allied forces protecting the capital city of Saigon. Rocket attacks and infantry

Below: An M60 machine gunner and his crewman lay down suppressing fire during combat in Hue City, Vietnam, allowing riflemen to advance.

assaults erupted throughout South Vietnam, including a successful penetration of Viet Cong forces into Hue City. At Hue, North Vietnamese regular forces gained control of the city and engaged U.S. Marines and South Vietnamese troops in 30 days of costly combat.

As what came to be known as the Tet Offensive raged throughout the south, Marines were also defending the strategically important air base of Khe Sanh against a North Vietnamese assault in what would become the longest communist siege of the war, from January through March of 1968. In the end, the North Vietnamese assault was blunted by massive air raids and determined infantry resistance from the Marines, as well as a relief operation led by the U.S. Army's 1st Air Cavalry Division. Clashes with communist forces in Southeast Asia continued through 1975, when U.S. forces and their allies withdrew from Vietnam, leaving the country to become reunified with the communist North.

A total of 13,091 Marines died during the fighting between 1964 and 1973; more than 51,000 Marines were wounded.

Above: During the Vietnam War the U.S. Marines received their first 5.56mm M16 rifles, which replaced the M14 as the primary service rifle. A version of the M16 remains in service today.

Operations Other Than War

As the Cold War continued, Marines became involved in more specialized missions. For example, in 1980, Marine Corps forces participated in a hostage-rescue raid called Desert One, which was an attempt to free U.S. citizens (including 13 Marines) held at the U.S. embassy in Tehran, Iran, by Islamic militants. Desert One failed when a helicopter and refueling plane collided, but the mission was characteristic of the "operations other than war" in which Marines were increasingly called upon to perform through the 1980s and 1990s. On October 23, 1983, a Marine Corps headquarters building in Beirut, Lebanon—part of a U.N. peacekeeping force placed there to defuse a civil war— was attacked with a terrorist group's truck bomb, killing 241 U.S. citizens,

Right: Sikorsky RH-53 helicopters aboard the aircraft carrier USS *Nimitz* on the eve of the failed attempted rescue of U.S. hostages in Iran, 1980.

including 220 Marines. In October 1983, a Marxist faction seized power in the tiny Caribbean island nation of Grenada, raising the concerns of the United States government and other states in the eastern Caribbean. With the encouragement of Grenada's Marxist coup leaders, communist Cuban troops and military equipment were moved to the island. Despite its small size, the United States and its allies viewed Grenada—with its modern airport—as strategically important during the Cold War. Later that month, the U.S. military was ordered to carry out Operation Urgent Fury, an invasion to topple the Marxist coup leaders and expel Cuban forces from Grenada. The operation included Marines and U.S. Navy and Army forces. In 1989, Marines and other military services formed an invasion force to oust Panamanian leader Manuel Noriega during Operation Just Cause. The U.S. government, which had previously supported the Panamanian regime, enacted a plan to capture Noriega after a series of crises further eroded democracy under his dictatorial regime, including a failed attempted to overthrow Noriega and remove him from power, violence committed by paramilitaries under Noriega's employ, and the harassment and murder of U.S. servicemen. The National Assembly of Panama declared war on the United States in 1989, and shortly after, U.S. military forces moved into the Panama Canal Zone to protect U.S. interests and people, and to destroy Noriega's government.

The Naval Reserve Officer Training Corps

There are Naval Reserve Officer Training Corps (ROTC) programs at more than 100 colleges and universities around the United States. Since 1932, the Marine Corps has been included in the Naval ROTC, wherein Marine officers are prepared for service while students in a regular academic program. The Marine Corps' goal is to hire 225 new officers annually from the Naval ROTC program.

The 1990s opened with a crisis in Kuwait on the Arabian Peninsula, as the U.N. resolved to oppose an invasion of this country by the forces of Iraqi president Saddam Hussein. More than 100,000 Marines were part of the ground and air assault forces positioned to defend Saudi Arabia's northeastern border and used to recapture Kuwait in Operation Desert Shield and Operation Desert Storm. Later in the 1990s, Marines were involved in humanitarian relief operations (providing food, security forces, disaster rescue, and other related capabilities) in a wide range of places, including Haiti, Bosnia-Herzegovina, Turkey, Liberia, and Somalia. Operations in and around the Somali capital, Mogadishu, as part of a U.N. force to enforce order and provide relief to **famine** victims, proved especially memorable, particularly for the U.S. Army Rangers involved in an intense firefight in 1993 while attempting to capture Somali warlord Mohammed Farah Aidid. Marines helped cover the final withdrawal of U.S. forces in 1994.

Left: The Marine in the foreground, pictured in Somalia in 1991, carries an M16 rifle with an attached M203 40mm grenade launcher and, slung across his back, an AT4 anti-tank rocket launcher.

Chapter 6
The Modern Marine Corps

Right: Though official military doctrine does not call for women to serve in front-line combat units, U.S. Marine Corps female recruits are trained as riflemen.

The Marine Corps has learned lessons from its history with amphibious warfare, expeditionary warfare, combined arms operations, and maneuver warfare to form the "Marine air-ground task force," or MAGTF (pronounced "MAG-TAF"), concept. MAGTF is the how the Marines are organized when they prepare for and go to war. The MAGTF, however large or small it is, usually includes a ground combat element of infantry and fighting vehicles, an air combat element with strike fighter planes and attack and transport helicopters, and a combat service support element for supply and maintenance.

The smallest type of MAGTF is called the Marine Expeditionary Unit. A Marine Expeditionary Unit is a **battalion**-sized force of between 1,500 and 3,000 Marines, vehicles, and the aircraft of a reinforced helicopter squadron. A Marine expeditionary unit carries 15 days' worth of food, fuel, and ammunition. Units of this type contributed to the war in Afghanistan in 2001 and 2002. During that time period, under what the United States military called Operation Enduring Freedom, the Marine Corps and the U.S. Navy formed Task Force 58, which worked with Special Forces fighting on the ground in Afghanistan. Task Force 58 was a **brigade**-sized group that included parts of the 15th and 26th

Below: In 2003, during Operation Iraqi Freedom, U.S. Marines entered combat more than 600 miles (1,000 km) inland of their starting point in Kuwait. Here Marines escort Iraqi prisoners of war.

Marine Air-Ground Task Forces

The largest-sized MAGTF, a Marine Expeditionary Force, includes between 20,000 and 90,000 Marines commanded by a lieutenant general. A Marine Expeditionary Brigade includes between 3,000 and 20,000 Marines commanded by a brigadier or major general. The typical Marine Expeditionary Unit includes between 1,500 and 3,000 Marines and is commanded by a colonel. The largest ground units organized by the Marine Corps include three active divisions with a fourth in reserve. Divisions are part of the Marine Expeditionary Forces. A regiment is a more traditional term describing a ground force of one or more battalions of Marines. A battalion is further subdivided into **companies**, and these into **platoons** and squads.

Below: A 1st Marine Division convoy moves up Iraqi Highway 80 toward Baghdad in March 2003.

Marine Expeditionary Units. Together, the 15th and the 26th Marine Expeditionary Units brought a ground combat element of between 3,000 and 6,000 Marines to Afghanistan. The amphibious assault ships USS *Peleliu* and USS *Bataan* brought Marines and their equipment near the coast of Pakistan.

U.S. Marine Corps Bases in Europe and Asia

This map shows the locations of major United States Marine Corps bases in Europe and Asia.

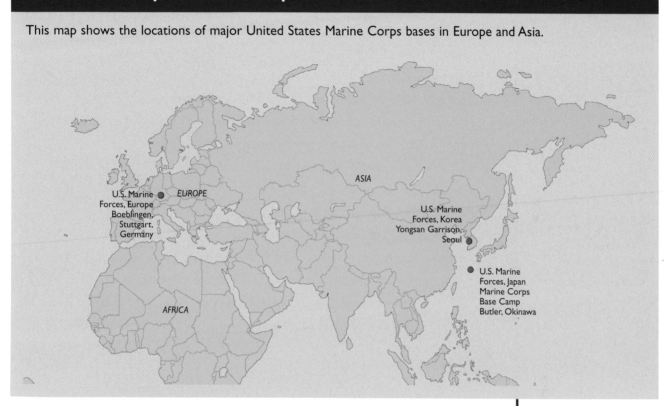

Navy landing craft carried the force ashore, and from Pakistan the troops and their vehicles were airlifted into Afghanistan.

A much larger MAGTF was brought to bear during Operation Iraqi Freedom in 2003 in which the United States moved to oust Iraqi dictator Saddam Hussein from power. More than 75,000 Marines participated in the war, including the largest form of MAGTF, called a Marine Expeditionary Force, which was brought into Iraq through the neighboring country of Kuwait. Marines who fought in Operation Iraqi Freedom traveled long distances during the war. For example, the distance from the Kuwaiti border with Iraq north to the city of Tikrit, located north of Baghdad, where the main fighting action ended, is 600 miles (1000 km)—about the same as the distance from Atlanta, Georgia, north to Washington, D.C.; and greater than the distance between San Diego, California, and San Francisco, California. To cover this distance rapidly and with protection, armored vehicles were a necessity.

Sexual Orientation

The U.S. military has attempted to develop a workable policy toward the sexual orientation, specifically homosexuality, of members of the uniformed services. The Marine Corps and other armed forces share a policy that forbids the persecution of persons who are homosexual. Noticeable homosexual conduct, however, may result in disciplinary action or in being dismissed from the service, according to the so-called "don't ask, don't tell" policy adopted in 1993.

Marine Corps Equipment

There are three Marine Expeditionary Forces in the Marine Corps today; each is a division-sized group that includes between 20,000 and 90,000 Marines and a full wing of more than 70 aircraft. The I Marine Expeditionary Force is based at California and Arizona; the II Marine Expeditionary Force is based at North Carolina and South Carolina; and the III Marine Expeditionary Force is based at Okinawa, Japan. The I Marine Expeditionary Force, and its largest subordinate

Right: The Marine Corps has come to rely upon the short take-off, vertical landing AV-8B Harrier II attack aircraft for close air support and strike missions.

unit, the 1st Marine Division, fought in Iraq alongside allied British forces in a version of the AMTRAC developed during World War II: the modern Amphibious Assault Vehicle. These tracked and armored personnel carriers, armed with .50-inch (12.7 millimeter) machine guns, carry 25 Marines at a top speed of 45 miles per hour (72 km/h). The 1st Marine Division also brought into Iraq a large number of Light Armored Vehicles—a sturdy eight-wheeled machine used for reconnaissance and fire support. There are several versions of the Light Armored Vehicle armed with a variety of weapons, such as 0.3-inch (7.62-mm) machine guns, a 1-inch (25-mm) chain gun, or a TOW II anti-tank guided-missile launcher. To overcome enemy armor, Marines brought their 68-ton (62-tonne) M1A1 Abrams main battle tanks into Iraq. These tanks, purchased after the Persian Gulf War (1990–1991), are armed with a 4.7-inch (120-mm) main gun, two 0.3-inch (7.62-mm) machine guns, and a .50-inch (12.7-mm) machine gun.

Heavy striking power also took to the sky during Operation Iraqi Freedom. Marine Corps aircraft flew more than 300 attack sorties per day during the war, many of these operating from Navy ships. The air wing attached to the I Marine Expeditionary Force included seven squadrons of F/A-18 Hornet strike fighters and five squadrons of AV-8B Harrier IIs. Four of the five Harrier II squadrons flew off Navy amphibious assault ships, such as the USS *Tarawa*, maneuvering in the northern Arabian Gulf. The Marine air wing also included 58 Super Cobra attack helicopters, armed with a variety of weapons, including a nose-mounted, three-barreled 0.78-inch (20-mm) cannon, 2.75-inch (70-mm) rockets, and Hellfire antitank missiles.

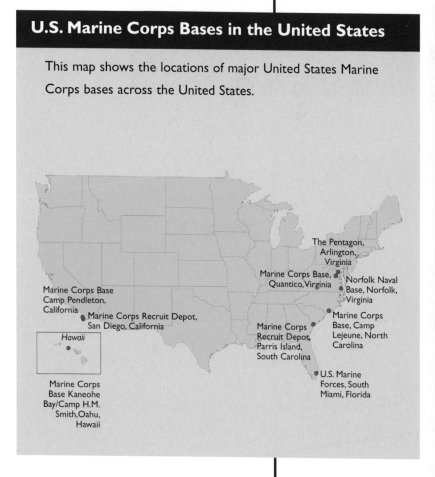

U.S. Marine Corps Bases in the United States

This map shows the locations of major United States Marine Corps bases across the United States.

The Pentagon, Arlington, Virginia

Marine Corps Base, Quantico, Virginia

Norfolk Naval Base, Norfolk, Virginia

Marine Corps Base Camp Pendleton, California

Marine Corps Recruit Depot, San Diego, California

Hawaii

Marine Corps Recruit Depot, Parris Island, South Carolina

Marine Corps Base, Camp Lejeune, North Carolina

Marine Corps Base Kaneohe Bay/Camp H.M. Smith, Oahu, Hawaii

U.S. Marine Forces, South Miami, Florida

As useful as the Super Cobra has been for close air support of Marine ground forces, they are vulnerable to enemy ground fire—49 of these aircraft were shot up during the fighting and needed to be repaired.

Marine Corps Tactics

Today's Marine Corps plans almost all of its operations, and trains to fight, as part of a team effort with other U.S. and allied military forces. The preparations for war in Iraq are a good example of how the Marine Corps works with others to accomplish its missions. For example, the modern U.S. Marine Corps works closely with special operations forces as was the case during Operation Iraqi Freedom. Before any deployment, a Marine Expeditionary Unit usually receives special training in order to earn the label "special operations-capable." These units can accomplish many of the same types of missions Special Forces accomplish, including reconnaissance; demolitions; aircrew rescue; the search and seizure of offshore fossil-fuel platforms; board, search, and seizure of vessels; and hostage rescue. Marines go through six months of intensive training in order to be certified as special-operations capable.

Marine Corps Training

The Marine Corps has long prided itself on recruit and officer training programs that exceed the requirements of other U.S. military services. To become one of "'the few, the proud," as Marines say, a recruit endures 13 weeks of physically demanding and mentally challenging boot camp at one of two places: Marine Corps Recruit Depot Parris Island, South Carolina, for those living on or near the East Coast, or Marine Corps Recruit Depot San Diego, California, for those near the West Coast. The Corps trains male and female recruits in separate, though equally challenging, programs. All female recruits, regardless of where they live in the United States, are schooled at Parris Island, South Carolina. Drill instructors preside at the depots over a regimen of

Above: During the toughest phase of training, known as "the crucible," U.S. Marine recruits practice teamwork to overcome an obstacle in a chemical contamination simulation.

training that is designed to instill strict discipline and **camaraderie** in each new Marine. Recruits must demonstrate proficiency with basic infantry fighting tactics, regardless of the job they may have later in their career, as the service prides itself on noting "every Marine [is] a rifleman." Finally, all Marine recruits must also pass through "the Crucible," a 54-hour-long ordeal during the last phase of training that tests a Marine's ability to go without food and sleep and to accomplish tough physical challenges, such as a 40-mile (64-km) road march.

The modern U.S. Marine Corps currently includes more than 156,000 enlisted Marines in active service and more than 18,000 officers in active service. The Marine Corps reserve force consists of about 36,000 enlisted Marines and almost 4,000 officers. There are almost 11,000 female Marines and more than 25,000 African American U.S. Marines in active service. The Corps also counts almost 32,000 persons of Hispanic or other backgrounds in active service.

Table of Ranks

Rank	Grade	Rank	Grade
General (4-Star)	O-10	Chief Warrant Officer – 3	CWO-3
Lieutenant General (3-Star)	O-9	Chief Warrant Officer – 2	CWO-2
Major General (2-Star)	O-8	Warrant Officer – 1	WO-1
Brigadier General (1-Star)	O-7	Sergeant Major / Master Gunnery Sergeant	E-9
Colonel	O-6	1st Sergeant / Master Sergeant	E-8
Lieutenant Colonel	O-5	Gunnery Sergeant	E-7
Major	O-4	Staff Sergeant	E-6
Captain	O-3	Sergeant	E-5
First Lieutenant	O-2	Corporal	E-4
Second Lieutenant	O-1	Lance Corporal	E-3
Chief Warrant Officer – 5	CWO-5	Private First Class	E-2
Chief Warrant Officer – 4	CWO-4	Private	E-1

The Marine Corps' most senior officer is the Commandant of the Marine Corps, a 4-star General. The Marines' most senior enlisted leader is the Sergeant Major of the Marine Corps. As a component of the Department of the Navy, the Marine Corps is administered under the senior civilian leadership of the Secretary of the Navy.

Time Line

1775:	November 10, the Continental Congress creates the U.S. Marines.
1783:	April, the Treaty of Paris disbands the U.S. Marines.
1798:	July 11, President John Adams establishes the U.S. Marine Corps.
1805:	April 27, First Lieutenant Presley O'Bannon captures Derne, Tripoli.
1901:	July, Private Dan Daly defends the U.S. Legation in Beijing, China.
1918:	June 6–26, the Marines defeat the Germans at Belleau Wood; August 13, Opha Mae Johnson becomes the first woman in the Marine Corps.
1942–1943:	Marines capture and hold Guadalcanal.
1945:	February 19–March 16, Marines take Mount Suribachi on Iwo Jima; April 1–June 21, Okinawa is captured.
1950:	September 15, Marines land at Inchon, Korea.
1968:	January 21–March 30, the siege of Khe Sanh, South Vietnam, takes place.
1980:	April 24, Desert One, the hostage rescue attempt in Iran, takes place.
1983:	October 23, a truck bomb is detonated outside a Marine Corps headquarters in Beirut, Lebanon, killing 241 U.S. citizens, including 220 Marines.
1983:	October 25, Marines take part in Operation Urgent Fury, the invasion of Grenada.
2001:	The Marines are involved in defense-related activities following the September 11 attacks.
2003:	Operation Iraqi Freedom takes place.

Glossary

abolitionist: someone who advocates the ending of slavery

arsenal: a collection of weapons

bastion: a fortified area or position

battalion: a military unit comprising three or more companies

bloc: a group of nations with a common interest or purpose

brigade: a large military unit comprising two or more regiments

camaraderie: spirit of friendly good-fellowship

communist: someone who believes in a (usually totalitarian) system of government in which a single authoritarian party controls state-owned means of production

company: a body of troops including two or more platoons and a headquarters

deploy: to place a military unit in battle formation, or to send a military unit overseas

division: a military unit larger than a regiment, capable of acting independently under one command

famine: an extreme scarcity of food

fortification: something that defends or strengthens

infantry: soldiers trained to fight on foot

legation: the official residence of a diplomatic minister

light infantry: lightly-armed, mobile, and agile troops

mortar: a muzzle-loading cannon with a short tube

mutiny: a concentrated revolt (as of a naval crew) against discipline or a superior officer

platoon: a military unit comprising two or more squads, or sections

regiment: a military unit comprising two or more battalions

secede: to withdraw from an organization

sortie: one mission by a single military plane

tribute: a payment by one ruler or nation to another in acknowledgment of submission or as the price of protection

Further Information

Books:

Aaseng, Nathan. *The Marine Corps in Action.* Berkeley Heights, NJ: Enslow Publishers, Inc., 2001.

Abramovitz, Melissa. *The U.S. Marine Corps at War.* Mankato, MN: Capstone Press, 2001.

Cooper, Jason. *U.S. Marine Corps.* Vero Beach, FL: The Rourke Book Company, Inc., 2003.

Kennedy, Robert C. *Life in the Marines.* New York: Children's Press, 2000.

Santella, Andrew. *Navajo Code Talkers.* Minneapolis: Compass Point Books, 2004.

Web sites:

United States Marine Corps Scholarship Foundation

www.marine-scholars.org/

Information on scholarships for the children of Marines or former Marines.

The U.S. Marine Corps

www.usmc.mil/

History, facts, and links to information about the Marine Corps.

The Marine Corps Systems Command

www.marcorsyscom.usmc.mil/

Marine Corps equipment and technology development center, describing new weapons-development projects.

United States Marine Corps

http://marines.com/

The official site for the USMC.

Marine Corps Recruit Depot

www.mcrdpi.usmc.mil/

The web site for Parris Island; provides information on training, recruiting commands, and more.

Index

Page numbers in **bold** indicate photographs or illustrations